When I die slingshot my ashes onto the surface of the moon

Jennifer Nguyen

First published 2019
by Subbed In
www.subbed.in

© Jennifer Nguyen 2019

Book design by Michael Sun
Cover design by Dan Hogan
Original template by Sam Wieck
Text set in 8pt Domaine Text

First edition

Printed and bound in Birraranga (Melbourne)

National Library of Australia Cataloguing-in-Publication:
Nguyen, Jennifer
When I die slingshot my ashes onto the surface of the moon / Jennifer Nguyen
ISBN: 978-0-6481475-6-5 (paperback)

Subbed In 007

All rights reserved.

This book is copyright. Apart from any fair dealing for the purposes of research, criticism, study, review or otherwise permitted under the Copyright Act, no part of this book may be reproduced by any process without permission. Inquiries should be addressed to Subbed In: hello@subbed.in

For my family
(both blood
and chosen)

These poems were written, printed, and bound on the stolen lands of the Wurundjeri, Woi murrung and Boonwurrung people of the Kulin nation whose sovereignty was never ceded. Jennifer Nguyen and Subbed In pay their respects to elders past and present. We extend warmth and solidarity to the Cadigal-Wangal people of the Eora Nation where this book was edited and designed.

Always was, always will be Aboriginal land.

8	Sometimes, pain is just pain
11	Humid for days
13	Backwards things
15	When I die slingshot my ashes onto the surface of the moon
18	"Ba, Mẹ ... I want to become a writer. I want to write for the rest of my life."
21	Death drives
24	I am always doing the leaving
26	Love at first laugh
28	ASTIGMATISM
30	my room smells like salt
32	Immortal wound
34	Time as best friend and worst enemy
36	Ode to my wall of empty wine bottles
38	Friday 11 May 2018
40	My misery doesn't love company
42	Venus Bay Beach No. 5
44	I thought a ghost was outside the bathroom door while I took a shit
46	HOW TO COPE
48	The trick is to think you are not an exception, that it happens to everyone, too
50	End of time
52	The zebra stripes on the back of the world prove that everything is essential, including you, including me
54	Quiet love scenario
56	Soft truths about you & I
58	Let me be
60	Paper boat hat
62	Red heaven
64	Let us build
66	Narcissus, daffodil; i grow numb
68	Requiem for a forgotten dream
70	The other day I saw an old friend. She said, 'How are you?'. I said, 'I'm good. How are you?'. She said, 'I'm good, too.'. Then, we went our separate ways.

Sometimes, pain is just pain

You said so yourself. So forgive me, these smiling tears.
One time I stapled my finger
and didn't even notice. These days
I write in colour because I can and it makes me happy.

The problem isn't that we don't have enough time. It's that
I thought, at the very least,
we'd have more time than this.

I had everything I needed as a child in order
to become a happy, well-adjusted adult.
          So .... why am I this way?

You read lines I etched into myself and interpreted that despite it all
       I wanted to live.
              I kept a garden of weeds
because they were beautiful to me. I didn't want to spray pesticide
                because insects are alive and need to eat, too.

At the beach I picked broken shells instead of pipis because other
people were already picking enough & if I said it hurt me to pick
a living thing, that we should leave now, go someplace else, do
something else, I would've probably become
          a happy, well-adjusted adult. So .... why am I this way?

        Is it because my parents never once said 'I love you'.
        I asked and wasn't happy with 'of course'.
        You asked me if I loved you. I said 'always', but you still
            left anyway.

All the places we used to go have gone out of business and become
something else.
You call me here and there, each time with nothing but news of the
death of someone
I once cared for and loved too,   even if they became my family last.

Sometimes, pain is just pain.

One time I stapled my finger and didn't even notice.
I did it a second time just to find out what happened exactly during the first.

> I know what you're thinking right now,
> what names and labels you have for me.

Sometimes, pain is just pain, but maybe with some time it can become something else.

> If I plant 100 seeds, maybe
> a few will bloom.
>
> If I write these words down, maybe
> they'll become a version small enough to swallow.
>
> If I learn a language and stop partway, maybe
> at least I'd know how to say *hi* and *bye*, and *please* and *thank-you*, and *I love you*, and *sorry, I'm sorry, I'm so sorry.*

Humid for days

Been living
on a steady diet of waffle cones stuffed full
of cookies & cream ice cream
and other times rum & raisin.

Been thinking a lot
about the piles of regret   living in the corners of my room,
in the margins of my notebook,   living in the pores of my skin
secreting a sebum they've yet to make a product for.

Been humid for days
my air-con timer set for 30 minutes straight. Last night
woke up four five times to reset it
and eventually trapped myself in a nightmare where

> ≠ ≠ earth sweltered from the heat and we all
> had to retreat underground. People would
> escape to the surface only to be evaporated
> to ash. Their ghosts would come back and say
> something along the lines of: *it was worth it,*
> *worth it to feel the real light of sun, to know*
> *nature, the goddess, still exists, even if it was*
> *only for a fragment of a moment* ≠ ≠

— I woke up
and even though I am afraid of lightning and thunder,
I sincerely wished
for the storm to come, anyway.

Backward things

Like   catching a cold in summer or
    leaving the fan on in winter

Writing about love
       grief
       moving on
               when you clearly haven't

More backward things like
       solving a math problem when you don't know what the numbers mean
       staying up late when you're clearly tired
       pushing yourself when you're already exhausted
       trying to change someone's mind when their mind has already been made up

In Thailand, in the back of an off-white pickup truck, I descended down a mountain
whose name I don't remember because it was 4 a.m. and I was tired
       but, I can tell you every single song I listened to that day
       as well as what the clouds were doing
Alright, so I can't tell you all the things you want to hear, but I can tell myself
       and that's not backwards   that's enough
All you need to know is I sat backwards and for once
       watched myself do the leaving
All you need to know is whenever conversations about peace or happiness come up
I think about this backwards ride down this mountain whose name I don't know
       I was with people but alone
       I was tired but didn't want to close my eyes   in case   I missed something important
       I wanted to know the name of the mountain
but my voice couldn't compete with the wind

When I die
slingshot my
ashes onto the
surface of the
moon

The fox in real life is elusive compared to the fox in my
dreams. In my dreams the fox places its soft fur-face
in my cupped hands, looks at me without blinking.

Must our sorrows compete? The fact that you feel
sad at all makes me want to apologise over and over
until it gets awkward and I become a burden.

I've never thought of world peace as achievable,
only because then happiness would become
obsolete, but at least then no-one would get hurt
anymore (I think?) so I suppose (if it's true) in this
scenario, I'm the villain.

5:58 a.m. in bed. Hot water bottle cold. The ice-cream
truck's song's juxtaposed against the metallic scraping
of a nearby construction site. A nineteen storey
apartment the whole neighbourhood rallied against
but in the end failed, because in the end, money.

Someone I know said: 'Not all suicides are the result
of depression' and to this day, I'm still trying to wrap
my head around something I can't see because
I'm looking at it too closely.

'I wish Pluto was a planet again'
was the saddest thing I read today.

The moon was so big and full I figured I could jump
and probably make it.

The moon was so near and close
it made me want to dig my own grave.

If I roll down a Very Large Hill what will kill me
first: breaking all my bones or boredom?

In the face of death, I'll laugh. Like, finally ...
I called you and you said you were
on your way, ten years ago.

In my dreams, the fox and I waste eternity away
in a field of wildflowers. Rather than answer my
question of what is or isn't poetry the fox shows me
a video, a memory of my Father putting on lip balm.
I come to realise that's the most delicate
I've ever seen him. And if that isn't poetry, then
when I die, slingshot the rest of me too.

"Ba, Mẹ ... I want to become a writer. I want to write for the rest of my life."

Helping pay the bills and writing a short story about someone who helps pay bills — which one pays the bills?

'Do we follow the path our parents want us to? The path they worked hard to set up for us? How far can we stray before it becomes betrayal?' These are legitimate concerns. Questions with no answers, only grey areas.

'No. Didn't we also work hard? Aren't we still? Don't we also have our own happiness to consider?'
One time I tried to call the bank up and went 'umm, err …' when they asked me to answer my security question: 'What is your dream job?' Yesterday, I wanted to be a florist. Today, a music video director. Tomorrow, someone my parents can be proud of and don't have to lie about at the annual extended family gathering.

This thing society calls 'adult' — what is it really? I ask Mum, who is nearing sixty, and she says, *Fuck it if I know, ask Dad*, who I don't bother because he looks happy watching soccer on a TV he found discarded on the side of the road.

I'm starting to become a gold medal contender at snoozing my alarm. Most mornings I don't remember pressing snooze. The list of things I didn't do gets pushed onto tomorrow's me. A me I try to forgive and understand because we both live with the same aches in our bodies and the same bruises on our brain.

Other times I sleep well into the next day. I sleep so long eventually the cat comes home. Where has she been? What are all the things she's seen? Did she take any active steps in getting closer to fulfilling all her hopes and dreams?

She lies down next to me and I watch in awe because less than a minute later, she's asleep. What's that like? Sleeping right away and not, you know, staying up all night worried about the rest of your life, but also, plagued by all your past mistakes.

Death drives

Be like the fly undone all day. The bra strap that shows and gives no fucks

Be like my Dad who overheard me say I suffer from chapped lips and after work the next day presented me with a tub of Vaseline

Be like the new fancy microwave my Mum bought that cools my food down while I try to heat it up and who will loudly and shrilly beep at me when it's done

Be like the alarm on my phone that I snooze every morning without realising that I'm doing it and now I'm late and class is over and I've skipped twelve weeks in a row

Be like the floating bed my Mum picked up on the street and gifted to me. I went to bed high that night without having to smoke anything

Be like that one shot of vodka too much and now you're throwing up and some of it's splashing back up from the toilet bowl to remind you of just how shitty everything is

Be like that bottle of wine that tastes like shit but you gotta pretend tastes good, because damn, it was expensive

Be like a broken tea bag, leaves scattered to the wind, all in your mouth, clogging your throat, ruining your morning

Be like the cat that had to go on a diet (because doctor's orders) but stayed round (because everyone in the neighbourhood was feeding it) and Oh, how I love and miss that round boy

Be like the pool that claimed to be 1.67m but when I stepped in sunk completely under

Be like my 50-year-old Aunty who has a colourful disco ball in her car to delight all her little grandchildren but most of all, herself

I am always doing the leaving

I fear when I find the place I want to be it might be too late.

If I drop a skateboard off the top of a tower will it land on its feet or will the feather and the stone in perpetual contention of who has it worse: combust? Summoning with it the bird that births the egg containing a post-post life.

Isn't a pen that doesn't write properly, worthless?

Isn't a song with odd notes not only hard to listen to but made fun of?

What do we slouch towards?

Is it enough to put yourself out there or must there be a pitch, some angle, some marketing strategy, a selling point?

The fish that suffocates in water?

A dog is lying on the side of the road. Who is to blame?

The optometrist asks *number 1 or number 2?* I ask to see both again.

Today is a day where everything looks the same

Love at first laugh

On a date with a girl I liked, she said 'Isn't *The Walking Dead* just *Home and Away* but with zombies ???' I have never fallen in love so fast before.

ASTIGMATISM

I dream I am burying myself alive. I dream I am digging the hole. The smell and feel of the earth between my fingers so vivid I might be awake. In the dream I come home. The home I've always known but something is wrong. The phở is the instant-packet kind and Mother's legs are fixed. The dream ends with her finding my bones in the woods where trees live without sun and leaves. Withered. A version of myself nobody was supposed to see.

Drink milk, grow tall. Mother said so. I was twelve when I stopped drinking milk out of a bottle. Twenty-two when I needed to submerge myself deeper, darker for longer. This went on for a time. The same song on repeat. I get sick of it but it never gets sick of me.

Tell me time isn't the undoing of both young and old. Nothing wrong with wasting days away / on screens / in bed. Nothing wrong with wasting days away so long as you won't regret it later. Nothing wrong with regretting things later. Tomorrow I have an optometrist's appointment. I don't want to go and hear my vision's gotten worse. I feel pathetic making wild guesses. Consider it an art form pretending to see something you can't. If I don't see someone for a long time I forget what they look like. Whenever people from my past recognise me, they say I haven't changed. I'm always filled with disappointment when I hear that.

I feel older than I actually am. I feel young and old at the same time. I feel I have no right to complain. I look at my parents and feel I have no right to complain. I asked Father what birds do if it's raining and they need to fly somewhere. He replied, *they can't fly, they can't go where they'd like.* There are things I want to speak to my parents about but my Vietnamese is so shockingly bad, sometimes, I'm afraid I'm not even pronouncing my own name right.

my room smells like salt

seashells
pink purple white

some smooth
some coarse

a small broken piece
from a tea set

you & i
a rainy sunday afternoon

there is no sun
the seconds run long

the cat is asleep
& so are we

Immortal wound

Teeth not made for tearing
flesh. When we are born it's the lips
that do all the work. A bad parent
is still your parent.

How a mouth
houses teeth.

How flesh clings
like I do
to the hand that strikes me.

Time as best friend and worst enemy

I trust in time
   even when it betrays me
   even when I am suffering &
time seems to stretch on
   a second becoming an hour &
not in a cute way like when you're
   kissing someone
                        but more like
when you find out a dog is almost eighty
& that's why when you offer your hand
   he can barely lift his head &
hobbles over to you
                        blind, slow.

Ode to my wall of empty wine bottles

Wall of bottles

> so that I do not have to see others &
> they do not have to see me

Glass coffin

> somewhere to reside
> when I die

Bury me

> as I am
> flaws and all

Circle ...

> / a cage
maybe? //

Vacuum up months

> lying under cover

From my room I can hear

> the recycling bin being emptied
>
> the start
> of a new day

Friday 11 May 2018

It rained after a long time of not raining / like a lightbulb on its last legs / My tyres slipped on the tram tracks / casting me into an alternate dimension / where Father comes home / whole / The winds howl at night / humbles me / Trees are uprooted from ground they've gripped for years / An ambulance rushes past / the traffic clears / The rainwater tank becomes full / From my room I hear the sound of something falling in / then silence / then wind / then rain again / A paper in the mail appears / 'Have you seen this cat?' / He answers to Leo. / If you have / please / call me /

My misery doesn't love company

Like me,
    my misery prefers to be left alone
to wallow in its reality, not having to justify
    or explain itself. My misery
listens to sad k-pop playlists with nice backgrounds.
    My misery does reckless things like drinking a
bottle of wine and then popping off the fly screen
    of the second floor bedroom window and sitting on the ledge
chain smoking a whole packet of cigarettes.
    Much like me, my misery is shy, but tends to overshare
if the opportunity presents itself.
    Much like me, my misery has learned to take it a day at a time,
our victories where they come, like managing to cook pasta al dente.
    Likewise, my misery and I are very much alive and would prefer
not to be killed, either out of kindness, mercy or spite, rather,
    just allowed to be.

Venus Bay
Beach No. 5

Go slow
gravel path

Petrol station
where leaving
means waiting your turn

Roundabout filled
with white cloud wildflowers

Arrived in time for low tide
a dirt road winding
down a sand path

Water opened
a cat yawning

Mist hanging
heaven's relaxing

Throw my body
out to sea. See how faithfully
she returns it back to me

I thought a ghost was outside the bathroom door while I took a shit

    Turns out it was just the cat

I thought someone was following me home
    Turns out it was just all those other times

I thought depression was to blame
    Turns out I'm just like everyone else

I thought I peaked in high school but actually
    I peaked as soon as I left the womb

I thought I was wandering about in the dark but actually
    my body and brain
    refused to cooperate for months

Days spent in my room
    curtains and windows shut up tight, with no one to call
Friend
    except for a spider
    spinning a home
    in the corner of my room
    that eventually starved
      and died

HOW TO COPE

Told MYSELF I was a ROBOT. MEANT ONLY to get to the next day. A ROBOT doesn't NEED to SLEEP. Doesn't NEED to EAT. Doesn't FEEL STRESS. A robot is PROGRAMMED FOR A PURPOSE. Get THROUGH this semester. Get THROUGH this next DOUBLE SHIFT. A robot WORKS HARD, GETS RESULTS. A robot doesn't NEED thanks. A robot is a robot SO LONG as it tells itself this. A robot keeps being a robot even once its PURPOSE is fulfilled. OH, the PERILS of being a robot.

The trick is to think you are not an exception, that it happens to everyone, too

I've been left behind a lot. My high school class
    Who picked me last for team sports; friends crowded
Me out when we walked a narrow sidewalk; lover who left me
    At a train station I'd never been to before; Mother
Who drove away, a cruel joke, and I who chased after her,
    An even crueller joke. In order to survive
My own loneliness I had to form attachments to things
    With permanence like words arranged on a page, or the way
Characters in a movie say the same lines no matter how many times
    You watch it. Things with less permanence were fine too,
Like a pot of jasmine tea. I was thankful even if a bird
    Landed near me and stayed for a few curious seconds
Before flitting away.

End of time

At the end of time
there is a small, wood house

with a porch, chair and wind chimes. I heard
its song, even though all was still.

It was not a song to sing along to and yet
I sang. It was different but familiar like

Have you ever re-met the Stranger Bird
and actually remembered?

At the end of time
the wind chimes sung

I was a car
stuck between two trams on a narrow road.

The trams took no passengers
and stopped a horrid amount of times.

Cars rushed past
running right through alighting ghosts.

I don't remember a face
or when a person was born —

my only party trick is that I can easily remember
words to a song.

The zebra stripes on the back of the world prove that everything is essential, including you, including me

Every 30,000 years or so
                    the Earth flips 180 degrees.
Perhaps I was born
during a moment's disorientation. I was born
and I'd spend the next 30,000
years trying to get my bearings, right before
                    the world flips
back round again.

Quiet love scenario

The day I realised a person can leave
Behind their scent on a bed they

Slept in the night before
I went crazy with awe

At the level of detail
Life had to offer

It was the same month I gave up
On plants that gave up on me and instead

Began baking bread and choosing ribbons
Matching the personalities of my friends and family

One time, in the middle of the night,
I woke up with a leg cramp

You got up too, half-asleep, massaged
And stretched my leg out

The same hands that earlier had helped me
Knead dough when mine got tired

How much time passed
I'll never know

When I woke up
It was already day

You were asleep next to me
And my leg bore a dull ache

Soft truths about you & I

you made me learn what love is, then you left

—

the difference between PAIN and RAIN is a single stroke

—

I can't get over your death
because I still think about you in the present tense

—

love waits until it can't anymore
then it is either memory. or longing. or both.
whichever hurts more

Let me be

The tiny space between clasped
palms Peeled back skin on knuckles
know the tenacity of a brick wall The edge of a knee
loved by a cat's cheek

Let me know
your moods Which meals and foods satisfy you
Where you go to get away What you think happens
when we die What you yearned for when you were a kid

Let me read your books whose words
have never left you The final pages
that changed you forever The diary you never wrote
but carry around inside you

Let me see how your loved ones
love you How you fare when life's not
too good The home you grew up in
The one you've always pictured for yourself

>	What's in the fridge?
>	Where do we hang our clothes to dry?

Paper boat hat

I dream not to avoid you but
So we can meet again

You pointed to a flower
And called it a bear

You pointed to a bear and said
Beware. This winter will be long

I came to know that magic is just perspective
The next time you give me a glass half full

I might just throw it on the ground
Because shattering is music and

Sand exceeds time, exceeds space. Why. Look
At pocketsful I still have from an old trip

If I hear you all around me
What am I supposed to focus on?

What if at the first psych session I was told:
If the problems lie inside you, no one else can help

And believed it to be so. I started building a bridge
But realised I didn't know how

I built a boat instead
One out of paper, asking 'Is that okay?'

It's more than okay,
I can imagine you say
In the end
The grin you'll have when you realise

The paper boat doubles as a hat

Red heaven

for Jonghyun, after
Before Our Spring

Sky glows the colour of Spring, of Dante,
of Asuka and her Evangelion, of a diary.

I'd like to hear you sing a language I do not know.
Longing translates the way your voice shakes,
the searching smile in your eyes.

Let's meet before the darkness disappears.
Let's meet while the world
sleeps.

Let us build

With our own hands
& if we have to
Destroy with the same hands

A hope that holds
An even bolder hope
That knows
When to let go

When it's time
A tiny boat
Willing to go out
Into the night

To find
The faint shape of home
Humming

Narcissus, daffodil; i grow numb

a bad dream	where outside
seemed	so serene
inside	even my fears had fears
i was looking	through
to the bed of moss	underneath
where human shaped rocks	lay
asleep	a mass grave
tessellation	of space and time
out on the lake	i saw a single swan
exist	only from the neck up
it bent forward	maybe to eat
or maybe to drink	the water
no longer	see through
reflected	the swan
kissing itself	making a perfect circle

Requiem for a forgotten dream

wet dream met with dry between the legs /
the eyes / hope that doesn't give back but
most of all / endures / driving down a highway / but to where? /

               the distance only looks like more of what
                you've already covered /

steering wheel stuck / decorative brakes / hazard
lights that don't blink / instead / showers you
in confetti / gray box cars / people who could

               be anyone / maybe even someone you owed
               thanks to but forgot

The other day I saw an old friend. She said, 'How are you?'. I said, 'I'm good. How are you?'. She said, 'I'm good, too.' Then, we went our separate ways.

A friend's father's moonshine rearranges my insides, makes me vomit up the sun. Things I don't understand frustrate me. Things I don't understand placate me. World peace was not achieved just because one side said 'I quit'. Mercy in practice is a spectrum. I mean, a spectacle. The best and worst case scenario is not the same for me as it is for you.

I was hungry so I baked shoestring fries with kimchi, jalapeños and low-fat mozzarella cheese. I ate some and despised myself. A diet tip I received (but never followed) was to eat a donut while facing a mirror.

Once, an apple I bit into had a worm and my Uncle said that's how you know it's healthy :) Once, I had a dream where every nerve in my body unravelled to make a giant worm made up of thousands of worms stuck together, human centipede style.

My Doctor sighs when he sees me because of my long list of things wrong with me and the fact that his appointments are backed up by an hour meaning he'll either have a late lunch or miss it altogether. I ask the receptionist if I can see a female doctor instead and she scoffs rolls her eyes saying, 'It was a male doctor that delivered all four of my children. What are you, embarrassed?' Not at all, I say. It's true I'm not. I tell her, I'm simply looking for someone to understand all the bad poetry I write. She says that'd make a good Tinder bio. I tell her that's where I got the line from and that actually, it makes a terrible Tinder bio. Afterwards I got in my car and drove home not crying but also crying a little.

I cannot look at myself in the mirror for fear of seeing a hair where society deems hair shouldn't be. Someone in my creative writing class states they will not eat anything that is shaped like a circle. I wondered why that might be. I thought about the things I refused to eat and found the list to end before it began, mostly for fear of getting my ass handed to me by my Mother. My shellfish allergy is strangely quiet especially when guests are around and she is showing off her lobster, abalone and oyster recipes.

Here is the list of things I'm supposed to eat that I looked up by googling 'What to eat if you have PCOS': dark, leafy greens, soy milk, tofu, nuts and seeds, healthy fats and oils, fish, meat, veggies and other unrefined foods.

McCain recently brought out a new frozen pizza. Sourdough. $3.75 though I swear the other day day the sign read $3.50. I cooked some up and told my current friend with benefits that I ordered Gradi off Uber Eats. She believed me, but when she took a bite I saw in her eyes she knew it was all lies.

NOTES

The poem *When I die slingshot my ashes onto the surface of the moon* is dedicated to a full moon I got to intimately know in 2018 and the members of SHINee, their 6th album *The Story of Light-Epilogue*, the music video and performances for *Good Evening* and shawols.

    The poem *Red heaven* is dedicated to Kim Jonghyun and is after his song *Before Our Spring* of which the poem borrows and alters a line.

ACKNOWLEDGEMENTS

Thank-you friends who generously read some of these poems and gave feedback.

My thanks to Dan Hogan and Victoria Manifold for not only believing in my manuscript but for believing in me. Thank-you for all your hard work, time and warm guidance in helping me bring this manuscript to the world. Thank-you for all that you do at Subbed In. I am so, so, so happy my chapbook found a home here.

Thank-you West Writers Group.

Thank-you to all the students and teachers I met during my studies.

Thank-you Ba, Mẹ, Hân, Vy, loves, friends, family (both blood and chosen; close by and across oceans) for all the sacrifices, lessons, love and laughter.

Thank-you Kim Namjoon for making mono.

Thank-you dear reader for giving my chapbook and the poems within your time, attention, energy and space.

ABOUT THE AUTHOR

Jennifer Nguyen is a Vietnamese–Australian writer, poet and editor. Her fiction, poetry and non-fiction has appeared in Ibis House, Scum Mag, The Lifted Brow (online), Rabbit, and Lor Journal, among others. Jennifer has performed writing at West Writers Forum and Melbourne Writers Festival. She edits fiction for Rambutan Literary, is an editorial mentee at Djed Press and was previously a creative producer at Emerging Writers' Festival. Jennifer is a member of West Writers Group based at the Footscray Community Arts Centre. Twitter *@jennguyennifer*

ABOUT SUBBED IN

Subbed In is a not-for-profit DIY literary organisation and small press based in Sydney, Australia. Subbed In's program of publications and events aim to elevate the voices of trans people, people of colour, non-binary people, sex workers, women, people with a disability, LGBTQIA+ people, First Nations people, survivors, working class people, and anyone who finds themselves on the margins of the supremely white, cis, heteronormative, capitalist, colonial, ableist, patriarchal hellscape in which we live.

For more information visit: *www.subbed.in*

ALSO AVAILABLE FROM SUBBED IN

blur by the
by Cham Zhi Yi

HAUNT (THE KOOLIE)
by Jason Gray

The Hostage
by Šime Knežević

If you're sexy and you know it slap your hams
by Eloise Grills

wheeze
by Marcus Whale

Parenthetical Bodies
by Allison Gallagher

The Naming
by Aisyah Shah Idil

Girls and Buoyant
by Emily Crocker

www.ingramcontent.com/pod-product-compliance
Lightning Source LLC
Chambersburg PA
CBHW032049290426
44110CB00012B/1014